P9-DFU-245

The Chinese

Lorien Kite

CRABTREE
Publishing Company

CRABTREE
Publishing Company

PMB 16A, 350 Fifth Avenue
Suite 3308
New York, NY 10118

612 Welland Avenue
St. Catharines, Ontario,
Canada, L2M 5V6

Co-ordinating editor: Ellen Rodger
Content Editor: Virginia Mainprize
Production Co-ordinator: Rosie Gowsell
Cover design: Robert MacGregor

Film: Embassy Graphics

Printer
Worzalla Publishing Company

Created by:
Brown Partworks Ltd
Commissioning editor: Anne O'Daly
Project editor: Caroline Beattie
Picture researcher: Adrian Bentley
Editorial assistant: Chris Wiegand
Maps: Mark Walker
Consultant: Donald Avery PhD

CATALOGING-IN-PUBLICATION DATA
Kite, Lorien.
 The Chinese / Lorien Kite.–1st ed.
  p.cm. – (We Came to North America)
 Includes index.
 Summary: Examines the history, traditions and
contributions of Chinese immigrants who have come
to live and work in the United States and Canada.
 ISBN 0-7787-0202-2 (pbk.) – ISBN 0-7787-0188-3
(rlb)
 1.Chinese Americans–History–Juvenile literature.2.
Chinese Americans–Biography–Juvenile literature. [1.
Chinese Americans.] I.Title. II. Series.
 E184.C5 K58 2000
 973'.04951–dc21   LC 99-049115
                         CIP

Photographs
AKG London 20; **Brown Partworks** Library
of Congress 25 (bottom), 28 (bottom); **Corbis**
15 (bottom); Annie Griffiths Belt 5(top), 5
(bottom), 29 (bottom), 31 (top); Bettmann 14,
19 (top), 28 (top); Bettmann/UPI 30 (bottom);
Gary Braasch 17 (top)a Gunter Marx front
cover, 12, 22 (top); Michael S. Yamashita 25
(topa; Mitchell Gerber 31 (bottom); Nik
Wheeler 24; Phil Schermeister 23 (bottom);
Philip Gould 21 (top); Underwood &
Underwood 4 (bottom); **Duncan Brown** 4
(top); **E.T. Archive** 9 (top), 29 (top); **Glenbow
Archives, Calgary, Canada** (NA-3740-29) 16;
Hulton Getty 8, 11; **Jade Snow Wong** 27;
North Wind Picture Archives title page, 13,
23 (top), back cover; **Peter Newark's Pictures**
7(top), 9 (bottom), 15 (top), 17 (bottom), 18, 19
(bottom); **Robert Hunt Picture Library** 21b;
Ronald Grant Archive 30 (top); **Sylvia
Cordaiy Photo Library** Johnathan Smith 6;
Travel Ink Chris Stock 22 (bottom); Nick
Battersby 7 (bottom).

Cover
Muscians play at a Chinese New Year parade in
Vancouver's China Town.

Book credits
page 10:'Leaves from the Life History of a
Chinese Immigrant,' *Social Process in Hawai'i*
2 (1936). From *Sojourners and Settlers:
Chinese Migrants in Hawai'i*, by Clarence E.
Glick, published by the Hawai'i Chinese History
Center and the University Press of Hawai'i,
Honolulu, 1980.

page 26: *Fifth Chinese Daughter*, by Jade Snow
Wong, published by the University of
Washington Press, 1989 (originally published by
Harper, New York, 1945).
Photo: Jade Snow Wong at the Mills College
Greek Theater, about 1943, when she was 21-
years old.

Contents

Introduction

The mid-1800s were a time of great hardship in China. Millions of people died of hunger in **famines** or were killed in wars and rebellions that tore the country apart. Millions more were forced to leave their country in search of work. Many of those who left sailed for North America. The discovery of gold on the West Coast had created a great demand for strong and willing workers.

At first, the new arrivals were accepted as a useful source of labor. They worked as gold miners, farm laborers, and railroad builders. They earned the reputation of being hardworking, smart, and dependable. Chinese workers played an important role in the opening up of both California in the United States and British Columbia in Canada.

By the 1880s, the good times were coming to an end. As the gold mines were emptied and jobs became scarce, anti-Chinese feeling spread throughout the Pacific Northwest. Violence against Chinese people became common. Laws preventing Chinese **immigration** were passed in both the United States and Canada.

▲ **Mann's Chinese theater in Hollywood, California. Many movie stars have signed their names and left their handprints and footprints in the concrete outside the theater.**

◀ **Chinese workers helped to build the railroads across North America. At first, the Chinese were employed by whites, but soon the Chinese began to put together their own work teams.**

The Chinese in North America formed organizations to fight **racist** laws, to support members of their communities in times of need, and to help new immigrants. Chinese districts, known as Chinatowns, sprang up in many cities.

A Chinese-Canadian girl dances to celebrate the New Year.

During World War II (1939–1945), when China, Canada, and the United States were **allies**, the position of the Chinese in North America improved. Canada and the United States gradually began to **abolish** their anti-Chinese immigration laws. By the 1970s, all immigrants were treated equally. Since then, new arrivals have more than doubled the Chinese populations of both countries.

Today, the Chinese in North America are a successful, confident community. Although new immigrants still face problems, Chinese Americans and Chinese Canadians have achieved great success in all walks of life. Chinese communities have kept many of their traditional beliefs and customs, and Chinese festivals are still celebrated on the streets of North America's Chinatowns.

▶ Chinese children, recently arrived from Hong Kong, share a music lesson with other children.

A Proud Heritage

Three thousand years ago, China had a system of government and a culture more advanced than any other country's. Paper, gunpowder, and the magnetic compass are three early Chinese inventions.

Today, there are over 50 **ethnic** groups living in China, speaking many different **dialects**. The largest ethnic group, the Han Chinese, make up over 90 per cent of the population. They trace their **ancestry** and **culture** to the powerful Han dynasty which ruled China for 400 years between 206 B.C. and 220 A.D. The Han speak many dialects of an original common language. Fifty-five minority groups make up the rest of the population. Each has its own language and culture.

Thousands of years ago, the Chinese invented a way of writing using characters, or **pictographs**, instead of an alphabet. Each object or idea is represented by a different character. Written Chinese has over 50,000 characters.

▲ For thousands of years, rice has been the most important crop in China.

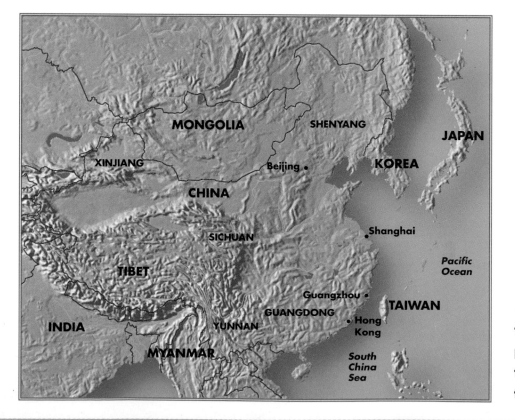

◄ For centuries, Chinese from the southern provinces have traveled to other countries to find work.

China has three great religious traditions: Confucianism, Daoism, and Buddhism. Each has influenced Chinese thought. Confucianism follows the teachings of a **scholar** named Confucius who lived from 551 to 479 B.C. He taught that people should be polite, wise, courageous, and show respect for their elders. Daoism is based on the teachings of Lao Ze, who lived at about the same time as Confucius. Daoists try to live simply and in **harmony** with nature. Buddhism spread to China from India about 2000 years ago. Buddhists believe that people must free themselves of worldly desires in order to achieve wisdom and happiness.

Many Chinese people also believe that the universe is made up of two opposite forces that work together to create a balance: one force is called *yin* (male) and the other force is called *yang* (female). In cooking, medicine, and many other areas of Chinese life, balancing the two forces is important.

Traditionally, learning has been highly respected in China, and the Chinese have stressed the importance of education. They believed that only scholars should rule the country. Almost 3000 years ago, the first schools were set up to train young men to take a difficult **civil service** exam.

▲ Chinese people from around 1880, including a peddler on the left, noblemen and women, and a barefoot soldier on the right.

▼ Pagodas were built to commemorate an important event or person.

A Time of Troubles

The first Chinese who came to North America arrived in the mid-nineteenth century. At the time, China's population was around 430 million. Farmers were finding it more and more difficult to produce enough food to feed all these people.

For centuries, China's rulers had looked down on Europeans. They strictly controlled European trade and travel in China. There was a great demand in the West for tea, silk, and other Chinese goods, but European merchants were allowed to trade only in the southern port of Guangzhou, and only during part of the year. China earned large amounts of gold and silver by trading with Europeans.

By the beginning of the nineteenth century, the gold and silver had begun to flow in the opposite direction. British traders were smuggling large quantities of opium, a drug produced in the British **colony** of India, into China. Millions of Chinese people became addicted to opium. Business and government stopped running smoothly, corruption and bribery were common, and the standard of living sank.

▲ A group of rebels in the Taiping Rebellion photographed in China in 1860. They are young and not well armed, although their big shields would have given them protection.

In 1839, Chinese officials destroyed 1000 tons of British opium to try to stop the trade. This action started the Opium War. For two years, British warships patrolled the coasts and seized several Chinese ports. The Chinese army was poorly commanded, badly equipped, and lacked discipline. Eventually, China was forced to surrender and sign a peace treaty. China had to open up four more ports to European merchants, and even more opium poured into the country.

Defeat in the Opium War was the start of a terrible period in Chinese history. Imported goods from Europe put many people out of work and weakened the economy. Poverty spread, and many people became robbers. Large parts of the country became lawless. Then in 1850, a great revolt started in southern China. Known as the Taiping Rebellion, it took the government 14 years to put down and cost 20 million lives. Millions more Chinese died as a result of famine and disease. Many Chinese people decided that their only chance of supporting themselves and their families was to travel overseas in search of work.

▲ Guangzhou harbor in 1767, when it was known as Canton. The flags show that Denmark, the United States, Sweden, Britain, and Luxembourg were trading with China.

▼ Chinese peasants worked hard, but many could not support their large families.

Eyewitness to History

ELIZABETH WONG was born in 1882 in southern China, near Hong Kong. Her family was so poor that her mother had to steal food to feed her family.

"In a small crowded village, a few miles from Hong Kong, fifty-four years ago I was born. There were four in our family, my mother, my father, my sister, and me. We lived in a two-room house. One was our sleeping room and the other served as parlor, kitchen and dining room. We were not rich enough to keep pigs or fowl; otherwise, our small house would have been more crowded than ever.

How can we live on six baskets of rice which were paid twice a year for my father's duty as a night watchman? Sometimes the peasants have a poor crop; then we go hungry. During the day my father would do other small jobs for the peasants or carpenters. My mother worked hard too for she went every day to the forest to gather wood for our stove....

Sometimes we would go hungry for days. My mother and me would go over the harvested rice fields of the peasants to pick the grains they dropped. Once in a while my mother would go near a big pile of grain and take a handful. She would then sit on them until the working men went home. As soon as they go we ran home. She clean and cook the rice for us two. We had only salt and water to eat with rice. "

Sailing for Gold Mountain

In 1848, gold was discovered in California. Rumors began to spread through China about a land of opportunity across the Pacific. The United States, and later Canada, became known as "Gold Mountain."

Over two million people left China between 1845 and 1900. Most of the early **emigrants** were from Guangdong province in southern China, where the people had suffered from war, disease, and famine. Emigrants traveled in small boats to Hong Kong. From there, some set out on the two-month journey to North America. Others went to Southeast Asia, South America, the West Indies, Australia, and New Zealand.

The first problem these emigrants faced was raising money for their fare. Some borrowed the money for their passage from shipping companies or future employers, such as **plantations**, mines, or railroad companies. Once they started working, a part of their wages would be deducted each month until they had repaid their debt.

▲ **Chinese prospectors placed a sign in Chinese on their house in the goldrush town of Barkerville, near the Fraser River in British Columbia, Canada.**

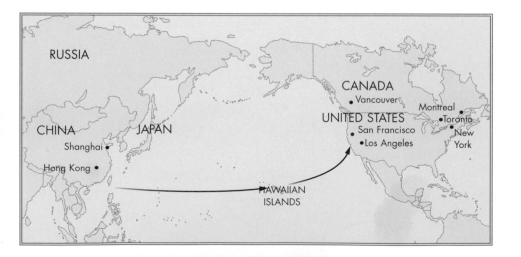

◄ **Many Chinese immigrants settled on the west coast of North America, in cities such as Vancouver, San Francisco, and Los Angeles.**

12

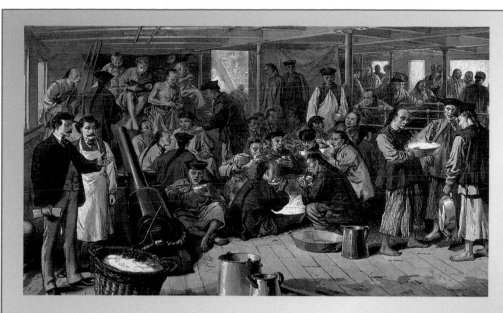

◄ Chinese immigrants to the United States cook a meal below deck on the steamship *Alaska*.

The Coolie Trade

By the middle of the nineteenth century, the slave trade had been abolished in most countries. There was still a great demand for cheap workers, and employers all over the world saw China as the ideal source. The word "coolie" comes from a Chinese word meaning "embittered labor." Coolie was the name given by Westerners to Chinese contract laborers — workers who signed contracts to work in distant lands for a fixed period of up to eight years. Western merchants employed Chinese agents to **recruit** laborers. These agents were paid only if they recruited enough men, so they often kidnapped people or tricked them into signing contracts. Just in case they changed their minds, contract laborers were kept in dockside prisons known as barracoons until their ships were about to depart. Many people died during the journey as a result of overcrowding and poor food. Those who survived often had to work under terrible conditions.

Other Chinese traveled as free men, hoping to make their fortunes in the gold fields or open businesses serving the Chinese community. Some used their own savings or sold property to pay for their tickets. Others borrowed money from friends or relatives.

Most of the emigrants were male. Some were single, but many emigrants left behind their wives and their children. These men hoped to support their families by sending home some of the money they earned. One thing that all shared, whether they were gold miners, merchants, or laborers, was the belief that their stay in North America would be only temporary. Their hearts were in China, and they dreamed of returning to their villages as rich men.

Land of Opportunity

The discovery of gold in 1848 changed California. Over 100,000 people flocked there in 1849, and by 1860 the population had grown to 400,000.

▲ Chinese immigrants panning for gold in California in the mid-nineteenth century.

The boom created by the gold rush led to a labor shortage. At first, the Chinese workers were welcomed because they were known to be hard working and reliable.

Not all the Chinese who came to North America were miners. Some came to work as cooks in mining camps. Others took any job they could get in the new gold-rush towns springing up all along the west coast. Merchants, imported food and supplies all the way from China and made huge profits.

Life in North America was very different from life in China. The climate and character of the west coast of North America is nothing like that of southern China. The immigrants' traditional clothes (short cotton jackets, light cotton trousers, and soft-soled cloth shoes) were too light for Californian winters. In addition, the Chinese saw North America as **primitive**, with the hastily constructed towns of the western frontier. Many Chinese, who had left their families and friends behind, felt lonely and lost.

▲ **In a San Francisco saloon bar, Chinese workers, recognizable by their hats and pigtails, mixed with Mexican and European men.**

By 1870, there were over 15,000 Chinese miners working on the west coast. Many had grown rich, at least by Chinese standards. Most worked riverbeds and diggings abandoned or sold by white miners. One newspaper wrote that "old abandoned claims that nobody thought had enough gold in them to buy salt, have been purchased by Chinese and worked with profit." The other miners, jealous of their success, often robbed Chinese miners and drove them off their claims. Hostility grew as surface deposits of gold ran out.

Hawaii

Shortly after its discovery by Captain James Cook in 1778, Hawaii became an important source of fresh water and food for ships sailing between China and North America. In 1852, the first contract field workers arrived from China to work in sugar plantations. Others came to work in stores or as free laborers on Chinese-owned rice farms.

By 1898, there were 46,000 Chinese people living in Hawaii.

Life on the plantations was hard. The work was back-breaking, the wages were low, and the hours were long. Most of the laborers left to find other work as soon as they had honored their contracts.

◄ **Chinese sugar plantation workers in 1871.**

The Railroads

In 1860, the journey across the North American continent took several months. To open up the West coast, both the Canadian and U.S. governments decided to build transcontinental railroads, which would cut the journey down to a week.

In the United States, the job of building the western half of the transcontinental railroad was given to the Central Pacific Railroad Company. At first, progress was slow. The American Civil War made it difficult for the company to attract enough workers. By 1864, it had managed to hire only 600 men, despite having advertised for 5000. The population of California was still small, and newcomers to the state were more interested in gold mining and **homesteading** than the back-breaking work of railroad building.

After two years, only 50 miles (80 km) of track had been laid. The company decided to hire a small group of Chinese laborers to try them out. They quickly learned how to do the job, worked hard, and were reliable.

▼ The camp of a Chinese work gang building the Canadian Pacific Railway.

By the end of the project, there were 15,000 Chinese men employed on the railroad. Unlike white workers, the Chinese were expected to provide their own food and shelter. They worked from sunrise to sunset, six days a week, and were given dangerous work such as grading (cutting out hills to fill ravines and gullies) and handling explosives. Many lives were lost as a result of accidents, disease, and avalanches in the high Sierra Mountains.

Finally, on May 10, 1869, at Promontory, Utah, a Chinese crew from the west met up with an Irish crew from the east. The two lines joined, and the first transcontinental railroad was complete.

Later, between 1880 and 1885, about 17,000 Chinese laborers helped to build the Canadian Pacific Railway (C.P.R.). Once again, they were given the most difficult work and were paid less than the other laborers. The Fraser Canyon was the most dangerous section of the Canadian Pacific Railway. To plant explosives in the sheer cliff faces, workers were lowered in small wicker baskets to chisel away ledges hundreds of feet above the ground. Today, Chinese Canadians have a saying that for every foot of railroad through the Fraser Canyon, a Chinese laborer died.

▲ Some sections of the C.P.R., like this one along the Fraser River, were cut out of steep mountainsides.

▼ Chinese workers carted away rocks and rubble and handled explosives.

17

The Rise of Anti-Chinese Feeling

The railroads across North America made the journey west cheaper and faster and encouraged people to move. Settlers arrived just as the gold mines were drying up, jobs were harder to find, and wages were going down. Many new arrivals took out their frustrations on the Chinese.

Labor organizations complained of what they called "unfair competition" from low-paid Chinese workers. They were also angered by the fact that men greatly outnumbered women in Chinese communities. How, they argued, could non-Chinese workers compete for jobs with men who were willing to take lower pay because they did not have families to support?

The Chinese could hardly be blamed for being underpaid. Nor was the fact that there were very few women unusual among immigrant communities. Many Chinese men would have liked to send for their families, but they could not afford to, and they did not want their families to suffer the kind of hostility that they faced every day.

Prejudice against the Chinese was shown in many ways, from name-calling to outbreaks of mob violence. There were anti-Chinese riots in San Francisco in 1877 and Denver in 1880. In 1885, 28 Chinese coal miners were shot in Rock Springs, Wyoming.

There were many more violent acts such as these, and few of those who committed the crimes were ever punished.

▲ An old cartoon showing racist attitudes and fears in the mid-1800s.

18

In 1882, the U.S. government passed the Chinese Exclusion Act, making the Chinese the first group of immigrants ever to be barred from the United States on the grounds of race. In Canada, Chinese immigrants were forced to pay an entry tax or "head tax," which rose steadily from $10 in 1884 to $500 in 1904. Eventually, on July 1, 1923, known to Chinese Canadians as Humiliation Day, the Canadian government banned Chinese immigration altogether. Because of these laws, Chinese miners and workers could not bring their wives, children, and parents to North America. Some men never saw their families again. Since there were so few Chinese women in North America, Most Chinese men spent their lives as bachelors in all-male communities.

▲ The Rock Springs massacre of 1885, when 28 Chinese workers were killed simply for being Chinese.

Chinese Organizations

In the North American climate of fear and hostility, it was important for Chinese people to stick together. They kept close ties with other immigrants from their home villages. They formed district associations, which lent members money to start businesses and provided **welfare** in times of need. New immigrants could go to these associations for help in finding a place to live and advice on where to find work.

At a national level, the Chinese Consolidated Benevolent Associations of both Canada and the United States fought against racist laws. They hired lawyers to defend Chinese people in the courts. Both organizations were run by merchants who became the leaders of Chinese community.

▲ Rich Chinese merchants, from the late nineteenth century, wearing their traditional silk clothing.

The Paper Sons

In 1906, a terrible earthquake devastated San Francisco, the home of North America's biggest Chinese community. Buildings were toppled, and fires caused by overturned lanterns and stoves raged through the city. Over 700 people were killed, and thousands were left homeless.

For the Chinese community of San Francisco, however, the tragedy had a silver lining. All the city's files of birth certificates were destroyed in the fires that followed the earthquake. This fact meant that there was no way for the authorities to check whether a Chinese person had been born in the United States or China.

The important thing about being born in the United States was that these U.S. citizens could bring their wives into the country. Many Chinese men, who now claimed they were born in the United States, sent for their wives. Between 1907 and 1924, about 10,000 Chinese women entered the United States. At last, families could take root.

▼ Most buildings collapsed in the 1906 San Francisco earthquake.

20

Angel Island

In 1910, in response to the new wave of arrivals, the U.S. government set up an immigration station at Angel Island in San Francisco Bay. Thousands of Chinese people were held there and questioned until they could prove that they were who they said they were.

▲ **A poem carved in Chinese on the wooden walls of the Angel Island immigration detention center.**

It was the worst possible introduction to the United States. Men and women, including husbands and wives, were separated from one another and subjected to humiliating medical examinations. The rooms were overcrowded, the food was bad, and the days were long and boring. About one person in every ten was sent back to China. To pass the time, **detainees** wrote poetry on the walls of their quarters, expressing their pain and anger at their treatment. Angel Island closed in 1940 but has recently reopened as a museum. The poetry survives, preserving the memory of this history.

The earthquake also meant that many more young Chinese could immigrate into the United States. By law, the children of U.S. citizens were also citizens, even if they had been born outside the country. Many young men left China and arrived in the United States claiming that they were the sons of U.S. citizens. Known as "paper sons," they memorized the facts about their "paper" families during the journey across the Pacific to prepare for the tough questioning they would face upon arrival from immigration officers.

"Paper sons" lived a double life: they used their paper names with the authorities, but they used their real names within the Chinese community. Yip Jing Tom, for example, entered the United States in 1921 under the name of Sen Hin Ying the sixteen-year old son of a merchant. On his gravestone, his real name, Yip Jing Tom, is written in Chinese, and his "paper" name, Sen Hin Ying, in English.

◀ **After the earthquake, many Chinese men sent for their wives and children to join them in San Francisco.**

Chinatowns

The first Chinese immigrants worked as miners, farmers, and railroad builders. By the twentieth century, most Chinese worked in city factories, stores, laundries, and restaurants.

Anti-Chinese feeling pushed Chinese workers from the countryside to the cities at the beginning of the twentieth century. Because Chinese immigrants were not welcome in the non-Chinese parts of cities, Chinese-owned homes and businesses often clustered together in districts known as Chinatowns. Large Chinatowns grew up in San Francisco, New York, Los Angeles, Vancouver, Toronto, Montreal, and many other cities.

▲ **Musicians play in a Chinese New Year parade in a Chinatown.**

▼ **This ornate gateway is at one of the entrances to Vancouver's Chinatown. The street signs in many Chinatowns are written in Chinese as well as in English.**

▲ Chinese accountants in a California Chinatown. The man in the middle is using an abacus, an ancient type of calculator.

In the early days, life in Chinatown was hard. Homes were terribly overcrowded. Whole families lived in tiny rooms between, below, and above shops.

Chinatowns became a welcome **refuge** from a hostile world. Chinese people could relax and talk freely. They could eat Chinese food, read newspapers in Chinese, send their children to Chinese schools, worship in Chinese temples, and have their hair cut in Chinese barbershops.

Here, "bachelor" men, separated from their families in China, lived in organized households, known as *fang k'ou*. When they were too old for work, they retired to community-supported homes.

Chinese Food

The Chinese restaurants of North America have long been popular with both Chinese and non-Chinese diners. Most serve traditional southern Chinese food, because the first Chinese immigrants to North America came from the south. The food is famous for its sweet flavors and seafood, usually served with rice. Ingredients must be fresh and are either boiled, steamed, or stir fried. Food is cut up into small pieces and eaten with chopsticks. Light soups are also popular and are regarded as both a food and a drink. Some changes have been made for North American tastes. The Chinese fortune cookie, for example, was invented because North Americans prefer to follow their meals with a sweet dessert rather than a fruit. The proverbs inside added a touch of Eastern mystery.

Food is also important in traditional Chinese medicine. Nausea, for example, can be treated with food containing fresh ginger.

▲ A Chinese cook uses a large rounded pan, called a wok, to fry food — sometimes it catches fire!

Chinese or North American?

By the 1920s and 1930s, a new generation of Chinese, born in the United States and Canada was growing up. While aware of the racism they faced, they felt more at home in North America than their parents.

These young people belonged to two separate worlds. What they learned from their teachers and schoolmates was different from what they were taught at home. Often this caused conflict between parents and their children. Chinese mothers and fathers expected obedience from their children and wanted them to follow traditional values. Parents were often upset when their children brought home new ideas.

Young women, especially, enjoyed freedoms they would not have had in China. In North America, they could choose their own husbands and had a chance to work outside the home. Some young women changed their names to sound more North American — for example, Soo Fei could change to Fay, or Yoon to June. Some girls were angry with their parents because they believed that their sons education was more important than their daughters'. These young girls believed that boys and girls should be given equal treatment.

Most of these second-generation children read and wrote English better than they did Chinese. They spoke English all day with their friends. They wanted to be accepted as equals in their adopted land and believed that education and hard work would bring success.

Many were to have their dreams shattered. Prejudice against the Chinese was still widespread, and even with college degrees, it was sometimes difficult for Chinese graduates to find the jobs they wanted. Robert Dun Wu, the prize-winning author reported that his brother, a graduate of one of the best universities in North America, could not get a job.

▲ A group of Chinese-American girls carry the U.S. flag in a street parade.

▶ A Chinese-American woman does **tai chi** in a San Francisco park to keep herself fit.

Faced with this discrimination, the idea of "going back" to China became popular among some members of the second generation, even though most had never been there. Perhaps in China, they thought, their talents would be recognized.

Some did make the journey across the Pacific, but most remained in North America. Gradually, they saw themselves not as North American or Chinese, but as Chinese Americans and Chinese Canadians: people who were proud of their traditional roots but also greatly influenced by the country in which they were born and raised.

▼ A San Francisco Chinese family. The children grew up to be Chinese Americans.

Eyewitness to History

JADE SNOW WONG was born in 1922. A successful potter and writer, she described her early life in *Fifth Chinese Daughter*, which was published in 1945. Here, the 16-year-old Jade Snow tries to persuade her parents to give her more freedom.

" Both of you should understand that I am growing up to be a woman in a society greatly different from the one you knew in China. You expect me to work my way through college — which would not have been possible in China.

You expect me to exercise judgment in choosing my employers and my jobs and in spending my own money in the American world. Then why can't I choose my friends? Of course independence is not safe. But safety isn't the only consideration. You must give me the freedom to find some answers for myself.

Mama found her tongue first. "You think you are too good for us because you have a little foreign book knowledge."

"You will learn the error of your ways after it is too late," Daddy added darkly.

By this Jade Snow knew that her parents had conceded defeat. Hoping to soften the blow, she tried to explain: "If I am to earn my living, I must learn how to get along with any kinds of people, with foreigners as well as Chinese. I intend to start finding out about them now. You must have confidence that I shall remain true to the spirit of your teachings. I shall bring back to you the new knowledge of whatever I learn. "

The Tide Turns

North American attitudes to the Chinese changed during World War II (1939–1945). After the bombing of Pearl Harbor in 1941, China, the United States, and Canada were allies against the Japanese.

▲ Thousands of Chinese New Yorkers marched in protest against the Japanese invasion of China.

Suddenly, both at home and abroad, the Chinese were seen as friends rather than enemies. Chinese Americans and Chinese Canadians helped the war effort, raising money, enlisting in the U.S. and Canadian armed forces, and working in shipyards and aircraft factories.

Chinese-American organizations continued their campaigns against anti-Chinese laws and practices. How, they argued, could Canada and the United States fight for freedom overseas while they **oppressed** some of their most loyal **citizens** at home?

Many anti-Chinese laws were **repealed** during and after the war. In 1943, the United States lifted the ban on Chinese immigration and allowed Chinese people not born in the country to apply for citizenship. Canada did the same four years later.

▶ **A Chinese welder helps build a ship to carry troops and supplies in World War II.**

Turmoil in China

The Chinese in North America have always kept a close interest in political events in China. The Chinese **emperors**, who ruled China until 1911, regarded all emigrants as traitors. In reaction to this, many overseas Chinese donated money to the Guomindang, a **political party** that opposed the emperor and wanted to modernize China.

After the fall of the last emperor, the Guomindang took power, but many difficult years followed, including invasion by the Japanese and **civil war**. Finally, in 1949, the Chinese Communist Party under Mao Zedong seized power, and the Guomindang leaders escaped to Taiwan, an island off southeast China.

Reactions to the new communist rule in the Chinese communities in the United States and Canada were divided. Some people were enthusiastic about communist rule, while others supported the campaign to overthrow the communists.

在毛澤東的勝利旗懺下前進

▲ Chairman Mao, the communist leader who became the leader of the People's Republic of China.

In 1965 and 1967, first the United States and then Canada abolished the last anti-Chinese immigration laws. All barriers to Chinese employment in Medicine, law, and education were removed. Since then, many new immigrants have come from Hong Kong and overseas Chinese communities in other areas of the world. The Chinese populations of both Canada and the United States have more than doubled as a result.

Recent waves of Chinese immigration have been very different from the first. The majority of the early immigrants were farmers from the countryside, who intended to return home after earning enough money. Most recent immigrants are well-educated city dwellers. Nearly all see North America as a permanent home.

▲ A volunteer visits a new immigrant to make him feel more at home in Canada.

Here to Stay

The Chinese community is firmly established in the mainstream of North American life, although prejudice against the Chinese has not disappeared.

Education is highly respected in the Chinese-American and Chinese-Canadian communities. Parents continue to encourage their children to work hard at school. Many graduates have enjoyed success in law, medicine, education, science, business, and the arts.

As it has become wealthier, the Chinese community has spread out from the city centers to **suburbs** such as Monterey Park in Los Angeles, which is also known as America's first suburban Chinatown. Chinese Americans and Chinese Canadians are also less concentrated in the western parts of North America than they used to be. The largest Chinatowns in the United States and Canada are no longer in San Francisco and Vancouver, but in New York and Toronto.

Chinatowns are still very important to the Chinese community. They are centers of the arts, with galleries, theaters, and movie houses showing Chinese-language films. Chinese restaurants are among the most important employers in Chinatown and are popular with Chinese and non-Chinese.

▲ The Chinese-American film director Wayne Wang has made films with both Chinese and non-Chinese subject matter.

▼ The Chinese American Dr. An Wang with his 1965 invention, the personal computer.

◄ A dancing dragon is led through the streets in a New Year parade. Several people have to support this fancy costume. People also dress up as lions during New Year celebrations.

Chinatowns burst into life during Chinese New Year. Red and gold decorations hang everywhere, and spectacular dragon dances are performed in the streets. Exploding firecrackers add to the excitement. In homes and restaurants, families enjoy great feasts of special food.

Family life is extremely important to the Chinese. Many Chinese North Americans keep the old tradition of paying respect to dead family members. At the spring festival of Qing Ming, families burn paper imitations of money, clothes, and other goods to make sure that their dead relatives have what they need in the next world.

▲ Connie Chung is one of North America's most successful journalists.

Success Stories

Jerry Yang is a co-founder of Yahoo!, the **internet search engine**. The great success of Yahoo! has made Jerry one of the richest people in the United States.

The Chinese-American tennis player Michael Chang has alsp achieved great success. He turned professional at the age of sixteen and won the French Open in 1989 at the age of seventeen. He was the youngest person ever to win a **Grand Slam** tournament.

Connie Chung is one of the most experienced and successful journalists in the United States. She has won three **Emmy Awards**, two for best interviewer.

Bestselling writer Amy Tan has become famous for novels that focus on being Chinese in America, such as *The Joy Luck Club* and *The Kitchen God's Wife*. Wayne Wang has directed a number of successful movies, including the screen version of *The Joy Luck Club*. Chinese-Canadian fashion designer Alfred Sung directs a multi-million dollar fashion business that includes his own brand of perfume.

Adrienne Clarkson (born Poy), whose family came from Hong Kong in 1942, became Governor General of Canada in October 1999. This appointment recognizes the important contribution of Canada's Chinese community to Canadian society.

Glossary

abolish To put an end to.

allies Countries that have agreed to support each other.

ancestry Family line going back in time.

citizen A person living in a country with rights and privileges within it.

civil service The people who carry out a government's work.

civil war Fighting between two groups in the same country.

colony Area of land settled or conquered by a distant state and controlled by it.

culture A group of people's way of life, including their language, beliefs, and art.

detainee Somebody being held by customs officers or police.

dialect A form of a language used in a particular area.

emigrant Someone who leaves their own country to go and live in another one.

Emmy Award Prize given for an achievement in television.

emperor The ruler of a very large territory.

ethnic Belonging to a group of people who are racially and culturally similar.

famine A serious lack of food in a country or an area.

Grand Slam One of four big tennis competitions.

harmony A feeling of agreement and respect.

homesteading Building a home and farming the land around it.

immigration Coming to settle in one country from another.

internet search engine A computer program that searches the internet for documents on any subject requested.

oppress To use power cruelly.

pictograph A symbol that represents a word or an idea.

plantation Estate on which cotton, tobacco, or tea is grown and which requires slaves or cheap labor.

political party A group of people with similar ideas about governing a country.

prejudice An unfair opinion.

primitive Basic, at an early stage of development.

racist Against a race of people.

recruit To find people to do a particular job.

refuge A place of shelter.

repeal To cancel a law.

scholar A wise person who studies a lot.

suburb The mainly residential area of a city away from the center.

tai chi A series of flowing movements done for both relaxation and exercise.

welfare Help that is given in the forms of money, food, or shelter.

Index

1 2 3 4 5 6 7 8 9 0 Printed in the USA 5 4 3 2 1 0